CELINE DION

The Inside Story Behind The Ailment of Canadian Most Popular Artist, Biography and Everything You Need To Know

HOOVER FELDER

TABLE OF CONTENT

INTRODUCTION

Celine Dion is a Canadian singer, actress, songwriter, and businesswoman. Dion is well-known for her powerful, technically excellent vocals. Celine Dion dreamed of being a performer as a child, emerging as a teen star in the French-speaking world after her manager and future husband, Rene Angelil, mortgaged his home to fund her first record. After signing with Epic Records in the 1990s, Dion rose to international prominence, becoming one of the most successful artists in pop music history. Dion's international breakthrough came in 1991 with Disney's animated film Beauty and the Beast, when she collaborated with Peabo Bryson on the title track. Celine Dion was the highest-earning entertainer in the world between 2000 and 2010. Celine made nearly $720 million in total revenue when you combine ticket sales, record sales, product sales, and all other sources of income. $500 million of that total came from purchases of tickets around the world. Only her Las Vegas concert brought in $350 million of the $500 million.

CHAPTER ONE

FACTS ABOUT CELINE DION YOU DIDN'T KNOW

There's a lot more to the songstress than you might think.

Celine Dion is one of the best-selling artists of all time, having sold over 200 million albums worldwide. Her voice can be heard almost anywhere, and many of her songs have made musical history. While you may be familiar with her musical output, here are some facts about the icon that you probably didn't know.

Celine Dion is the fourteenth child in a family of fourteen.

Celine's mother, Thérèse Dion, wanted to be done having children after the birth of her twins (the 12th and 13th children), according to Celine: The Authorized Biography of Celine Dion. She was 41 years old at the time and was ready for some alone time (which was understandable!). She intended to get a job and travel with her husband. But when she discovered she was pregnant again, she was devastated "Her entire plan was thrown out the window. Her life, her husband's life, and the lives of all her children would be altered "author Georges-Hébert Germain.

She was born to be a star

Celine's extended family was certainly musical—her parents founded the group Dion's Family, which toured Canada when Celine was a baby.

Her family owned a piano bar.

The Dions opened Le Vieux Baril (The Old Barrel), a piano bar in Charlemagne, Quebec, and even lived on the premises. Celine began singing in the lounge when she was five years old. Customers quickly became aware of her magnificent voice and began making requests for her to perform.

Celine's childhood home was demolished in 2014, but it was replaced by a structure that now houses her charitable organization, Foundation Maman Dion.

At the age of twelve, she won her first record deal.

Before she was a teenager, she recorded her first song, "Ce N'est Qu'un Rêve" (It Was Only a Dream). Celine's brother Jacques sent the demo to Canadian producer René Angélil, who was at the time managing Canadian star Ginette Reno. Celine's mother included a note with the demo: "This is a 12-year-old with a fantastic voice. Please listen to her. We want her to be as successful as Ginette Reno."

Angélil, on the other hand, didn't listen to the tape for weeks; it was Celine's brother, Michael, who eventually met with him and urged him to do so; He then invited her to Quebec for an audition.

"While I was singing, he started to cry," Celine has said of the audition. "I knew then I had done a good job." Angélil signed her immediately. (Of course, the two married in 1994.)

She sang for the pope when she was 16 years old.

During Pope John II's visit to Quebec in September 1984, she performed "Une Colombe," a popular French song. The concert drew a crowd of 65,000 people to Montreal's Olympic Stadium.

Michael Jackson inspired her to become a global celebrity.

Celine had already won several awards and released nine French albums by the age of 18. Then she saw superstar Michael Jackson perform on television, and she told Angélil that she wanted that level of success.

Angélil had Celine take a year off to make it happen. She got a makeover, learned English, and began working on her first English-language album, Unison, which was released in 1990.

During her first American tour, she lost her voice.

During a Unison tour, she lost her voice during a concert. Following an earlier bout with laryngitis, as well as fatigue from a hectic schedule, Celine's vocal cords became inflamed, preventing her from performing and forcing her to cancel shows. She followed doctor's orders and remained completely silent for three weeks in order to avoid vocal cord surgery. She then established a strict routine to better care for her voice.

It almost never happened that "My heart will go on."

Celine's most famous song is, of course, "My Heart Will Go On," the Titanic theme song. The power ballad is one of the best-selling singles of all time, and it was named one of the "songs of the century" by the Recording Industry Association of America, but it was almost never recorded.

Celine initially disliked the song and refused to sing it. "I wasn't certain. I had previously done another song for a film that was very successful, and I thought we were pushing our luck "She revealed this to talk show host Jonathan Ross.

The song was recorded entirely in one take.

Angélil persuaded Celine to record a demo for the song despite her reluctance. The demo, which was completed in one take, became the version that the world fell in love with. "The demo is the actual recording; I never sang the song again. Except for three million times after that, "Celine stated.

She has an honorary doctorate.

Celine Dion became Dr. Dion in August 2008 after receiving an honorary doctorate from Laval University in Quebec. The singer, who never finished high school, called the honor "a very great honor for a little girl from Charlemagne." She dedicated the award to her husband for his contribution to her successful career. René died from cancer in January 2016. "In a way, my career was his masterpiece, his song, his symphony," she said at his funeral.

CHAPTER TWO

PERSONAL LIFE AND CAREER

A LEGEND WAS BORN

On March 30, 1968, in the small village of Charlemagne, Québec, which is located 50 kilometers from Montréal, Celine Dion was born. She was Thérèse Tanguay and Adhémar Dion's fourteenth child. The Dion family had limited income but was always full of affection. Celine's mother had to put her youngest child to sleep in a drawer since there were so many children living there.

The mythology had already started.

The same passion for music was shared by the entire family. Even the parents and kids got together to form a group that gave local audiences concerts. Celine has always participated, even as a little child. Thérèse saw her baby's extraordinary talent right away. Although Celine was extraordinarily gifted, all of her children were.

With the assistance of her mother and brother Jacques, she wrote her first song at the age of 12 called "Ce n'était qu'un rêve." But it's safe to say that it was real. And with the help of her mother, that dream would begin to materialize. Thérèse gave music mogul René Angélil a cassette of the song. She picked him because he had overseen the career of the family's favorite singer, Ginette Reno of Quebec. Reno had just told Angélil that she would no longer need his assistance. When he first heard the cassette that would change both his and the fate of a young girl from Charlemagne, he was ready to realign his career.

She was given a pencil and a microphone as he extended an invitation to meet with him in his office. As if you were performing for a packed house, start singing. Celine sung. René instantly became one of her biggest supporters. The best artist-manager relationship in show business history had just begun, and it was just the beginning.

EARLY SUCCESS

On Michel Jasmin's chat show on June 19, 1981, Celine Dion performed for the first time on television. The Quebec audience took to her right away. Everyone believed she would succeed, but no one could have predicted what would happen.

René Angélil had such unwavering faith in his young protégée that he mortgaged his home to pay for the recording of her first album. The great gambler made the best wager they had ever placed. Eddy Marnay, a lyricist who has collaborated with some of the best vocalists in the world, including Barbra Streisand, Yves Montand, and Édith Piaf, agreed to write songs for Celine. "It's the voice of the Good Lord!" Marnay shouted upon hearing Celine sing for the first time. Their first single would be La voix du bien Dieu.

Celine won the gold medal at the 13th Yamaha World Popular Song Festival in Tokyo in 1982. She performed "Tellement j'ai d'amour pour toi," written by Marnay and Giraud, in front of 115 million TV viewers. She was only fourteen years old.

Following that, she made her first appearance on French television, on the renowned program Champs-Élysées, hosted by Michel Drucker. To this day, the entire country remembers the moment when the host announced to his audience, "Remember her name: Celine Dion! "She was the first Canadian to have an album awarded gold status in France in 1983. It would not be her last.

That same year, she received her first four Félix Awards at the ADISQ gala honoring the best in Quebec music. She has a total of 45 victories to her credit.

On September 11, 1984, 60,000 people watched Celine sing "Une colombe" in front of Pope John Paul II in Montreal's Olympic Stadium. A grace moment. Two months later, she performed at the Olympia in Paris as Patrick Sébastien's opening act for five weeks. In 1985, she started a lengthy tour in Quebec. From concert to show, the young vocalist was becoming a great performer.

CELINE 18 MONTH BREAK

Then she and her manager decided it was time to take a break. Celine, a rising artist, took a break from live performance for 18 months. It was yet another risky bet. Will she be forgotten, like so many other child stars before her, unable to repeat their debut success? In fact, the inverse was true. When she returned, her fans saw a Celine transformed, more solid than ever, having perfected her English and topping the charts with the album that marked her transformation: Incognito. Luc Plamondon, a talented lyricist in tune with his era, wrote the title track. Celine was no longer a child performer; she was the voice of her generation. Incognito sold over 500,000 copies.

It was the first album released by her new record label, CBS, which later merged with Sony Music to form Sony Music Entertainment, the same label as Michael Jackson. Celine had made it to the big leagues.

In 1988, she won the prestigious Eurovision song contest in front of 600 million TV viewers in Dublin, Ireland. That was the start of her worldwide conquest.

She effectively tapped into the American market in 1990 with the release of her debut English album, Unison. "Where Does My Heart Beat Now?", a song. was certified gold in the United States and peaked at number five on the charts. Jay Leno, the host of The Tonight Show, welcomed her and predicted she would have a successful career. She won the Juno Award for Album of the Year and Female Vocalist of the Year at Canada's Juno Awards, which honor the best in Canadian music.

She released the album Dion Chante Plamondon in the autumn of 1991, which was certified gold on the day of its release.

A Walt Disney movie theme song let the singer fulfill her own American dream as her career progressed like a storybook. Celine and Peabo Bryson's duet of "Beauty and the Beast," which received Grammy and

Academy Award nominations, peaked at number one on charts all around the world. Celine performed with Peabo during the Oscars broadcast on March 30, 1992, her 24th birthday.

The night following the Oscars, Celine made the Tonight Show debut of her second English-language album. Celine was dubbed a "once-in-a-generation voice" by the Wall Street Journal.

MARRIAGE

The strength of love was what pushed the Dion-Angélil team, and Celine sang "The Power of Love" at the Kennedy Center in Washington, D.C., for President Clinton, as 1993 got underway. Following the publication of her album The Colour of My Love in November, Celine told her audience that she was in love with René.

For four weeks, "The Power of Love" held the number one spot on the Billboard charts. The album "Think Twice" and the single "Think Twice" both topped the hit parade in England for 5 weeks, tying The Beatles' record. After selling more than a million copies, The Colour of My Love received a diamond certification in Canada.

On December 17, 1994, Celine wed the love of her life, René Angélil, in Montréal's Notre-Dame Basilica. It was a meaningful and exquisite wedding fit for a princess. The mythology continued, as did her honeymoon with her audience.

In 1995, Celine Dion and singer-songwriter Jean-Jacques Goldman worked together to produce D'eux, one of the greatest works of francophone music. It would go on to become the best-selling French album of all time, selling 10 million copies worldwide, with a string of timeless hits like "Pour que tu m'aimes encore", "Je sais pas", "Les derniers seront les premiers"

The heartfelt ballad "Vole," which was dedicated to Celine's niece Karine, who passed away at the age of

16 following a protracted battle with cystic fibrosis, was also featured on D'eux.

In February 1996, Celine won the Victoires de la Musique, the French equivalent of the Grammy Awards, for Song of the Year (Pour que tu m'aimes encore) and Female Vocalist of the Year.

Celine released her album Falling Into You in March of the same year. It went on to become the best-selling album in the world in 1996. The album debuted at number one in 11 countries and went on to win two Grammy Awards, including Album of the Year. Over 30 million copies of Falling Into You have been sold.

Celine Dion performed "The Power of the Dream" during the Opening Ceremonies of the Atlanta Olympic Games on July 19, 1996, in front of 3.5 billion viewers on television. It was the ultimate triumph: she had become the world's most famous singer.

"Let's Talk About Love"

In March 1997, Celine Dion made history by becoming the first performer to give two songs at the Oscars. She performed her own hit "Because You Loved Me," the theme song from the film Up Close and Personal, and stepped in for an ailing Natalie Cole, performing "I Finally Found Someone," the theme song from the film The Mirror Has Two Faces. The woman has steely nerves.

Let's Talk About Love, Celine's 18th album, was released in November 1997, and featured collaborations with Luciano Pavarotti, Barbra Streisand, the Bee Gees, Carole King, and Sir George Martin. What a beautiful constellation of stars! Let's Talk About Love also featured the historic single "My Heart Will Go On," the theme song from the blockbuster Titanic.

She delivered it magnificently at the 70th Academy Awards. The Oscar for Best Original Song went to "My Heart Will Go On." The original soundtrack to Titanic became the best-selling soundtrack in history, selling 30 million copies, equaling the sales of the album Let's Talk About Love, which also includes the hymn to Jack and Rose's love affair. A titanic achievement.

Celine released her album "S'il suffisait d'aimer" in February 1998, co-written with her close collaborator Jean-Jacques Goldman. The title song quickly became a classic in the francophone repertoire. She gave her fans a gift just before the end of the year: the album These Are Special Times. George Hébert-Germain wrote her first official biography, which was published the same year.

The Let's Talk About Love world tour was a massive success, culminating in two evenings at the Stade de France in Paris, attended by 180,000. René, who is now battling cancer, was unable to attend the events. Celine paid tribute to him during the show and received a standing ovation. René overcame the disease and was onstage at the Centre Molson in Montréal on December 31, 1999, kissing his sweetheart in the final seconds of the millennium. Celine's extraordinary performance was her final before a well-deserved rest.

MOTHERHOOD OF CELINE DION

Celine took on the most important role of her life on January 25, 2001: mother! René-Charles Angélil was born at 1 a.m. and weighed 6 pounds, 8 ounces.

Celine released her album A New Day Has Come just over a year later. It topped the charts in 17 countries, including Canada, France, the United States, the United Kingdom, and Australia.

Then René, the visionary, took another risk that only Celine could win. He created a new show in Las Vegas in a 4000-seat theater specially designed for her in Caesars Palace, and presented it as a residency, five nights a week, for at least three years. Franco Dragone, the renowned creator behind 10 Cirque du Soleil productions, directed the spectacle, which included dancers and special effects. A New Day... is a revolutionary show. It changed the face of the entertainment capital for good.

The premiere took place on March 25, 2003, and the finale took place nearly 5 years later, on December 15, 2007. Over 700 sold-out performances for over 3 million people! The gamble paid off yet again. Celine Dion Live in Las Vegas became Canada's first triple-platinum certified music DVD.

During her residency in Vegas, Celine found time to release the albums One Heart, Une Fille, and 4 Types, as well as the live album A New Day... Live in Las Vegas, Miracle and D'elles concept albums, On ne change pas compilation, and Taking Chances.

She also managed to appear at the Oscars for the fifth time on February 25, 2007, in a tribute to one of the greatest film composers, Italy's Ennio Morricone.

Celine embarked on a new global conquest just as her Las Vegas farewell was coming to an end. Her tour began on February 14, 2008, in South Africa, and continued through Asia, Australia, Europe, Canada, and the United States. 5 continents, 23 countries, 93 cities, and a total of 3 million spectators. The tour was the second most profitable in North America in 2008. Celine: Through the Eyes of the World immortalized the world tour by portraying it as a family vacation. We follow Celine and her family through each stop. The DVD debuted at number one in Canada, the United States, and the United Kingdom.

On August 22, 2008, Celine triumphed in front of 250,000 fans gathered on the Plains of Abraham for a one-of-a-kind concert as part of the festivities commemorating Québec City's 400th anniversary. She sang many duets with each of her special guests, but most importantly, she finally got to sing with one of her all-time idols.

THE FINAL DAYS OF RENÉ ANGÉLIL

The world's best-selling female singer took a break for her second pregnancy. And, because she never does anything half-heartedly, she gave birth to twins,

Nelson and Eddy, on October 23, 2010! They were baptized on March 5, 2011, in Las Vegas, just ten days before her highly anticipated return to Caesars Palace's Colosseum.

Celine returned to the stage with a brand-new show directed by Ken Ehrlich, the Grammy Awards producer. Las Vegas has reclaimed its diva. The entire city walked a little higher. Her second stint at the Colosseum shattered all box office records. The show was ranked first in the Billboard Boxscore, the North American concert bible.

Celine released her new album Sans Attendre in November 2012, featuring duets with francophone song icons Johnny Hallyday, Jean-Pierre Ferland, and the late Henri Salvador. The album, which certified diamond in France, was the best-selling album in Quebec that year.

Celine released the album Loved Me Back To Life in 2013, much to the delight of her fans all over the world. It topped the iTunes charts in 44 countries and peaked at number two on the Billboard Top 200.

Celine returned home in July 2013, performing the concert-event Celine une seule fois on the Plains of Abraham in Québec City.

Then, at the end of 2013, René received shocking news: he had relapsed with throat cancer.

Several months later, in 2014, Celine announced that she was canceling all of her engagements in order to be closer to her husband, who was battling cancer. Celine returned home to care for her man and her family.

After spending several months by René's bedside, her sweetheart requested a favor: he wanted to see her perform again. He wished to hear her sing once more. As a result, Celine resumed her residency at Caesars Palace. By night, she's a diva; by day, she's a mother, wife, and caregiver.

Rene Angélil, the world's most famous impresario, died on January 14, 2016. Hundreds of millions of fans were in mourning. Never before had a man in the shadows held such sway over the people's hearts. Celine would suffer a double blow from fate when her brother Daniel died two days later.

Angélil was buried on January 22 after a national funeral in Montréal's Notre-Dame Basilica, the same place where Celine and René had been united, for better or for worse, until death do us part 22 years earlier.

Celine had received condolences from thousands of fans the night before, while lying in state. René's decisions about Celine's career had been guided by his concern for and desire to please her audience. The greatest legacy this distinguished man has left to the artistic community is respect for the audience and Celine is consumed by the same flame.

LIFE AFTER RENÉ

That is why, on February 23, 2016, several weeks after her husband's death, Celine returned to the Colosseum stage. She understands that her fans rely on her to light up their lives, and she relies on them to light up hers. The concert's start, as relayed on the Internet, captured the attention of the online world.

Celine performed "The Show Must Go On" at the Billboard Music Awards on May 22 and was presented with the Lifetime Achievement Icon Award by her son, René-Charles. Rarely has an award presentation been so moving, so full of tender and genuine emotion.

She released the first single from her new French-language album on May 24. "Encore un Soir," written by Jean-Jacques Goldman, is a tribute to René. The song soared to the top of every French-language chart.

Celine finished a 28-show sold-out tour of Europe and Québec in the summer before returning to Las Vegas for more shows.

Encore Un Soir Celine's first French-language album in four years was released in August by Sony Music. Encore un soir was certified Diamond in France, Double-Platinum in Canada, and Platinum in Belgium and Switzerland, and topped the charts in all four countries. Encore un soir was also Celine's first French-language album to chart in the United States.

Celine began 2017 by extending her residency at Caesars Palace's Colosseum in Las Vegas. Celine Dion launched the Celine Dion Collection, a line of handbags, luggage, and accessories, and released "How Does This Moment Last Forever," the theme song for the live-action remake of Beauty and the Beast.

Celine attended the prestigious Met Gala in New York in May, looking stunning in an Atelier Versace gown designed by Donatella Versace. Later that month, Celine performed her megahit "My Heart Will Go On" at the Billboard Music Awards to commemorate the 20th anniversary of the film Titanic.

Celine took a break from her Las Vegas residency in the summer of 2017 to tour across Europe and the United Kingdom, performing 25 sold-out shows in 15 cities. She broke records as the highest grossing artist at every UK venue and received critical acclaim.

Following her triumphant trip to Europe, Celine returned to Caesars Palace for a new season of shows to close out 2017.

The song "Ashes," from the soundtrack of the Deadpool 2 film, was released in May 2018, along with the official video, directed by David Leitch. The video features Deadpool himself and was shot in Caesars Palace's The Colosseum, which also houses Celine's Las Vegas residency show.

Celine embarked on a two-month tour of the Asia-Pacific region, Australia, and New Zealand that summer, her first in 20 years! Celine returned to the Colosseum at Caesars Palace in September 2018 and announced that her second production Celine at The Colosseum at Caesars Palace would close on June 8,

2019, more than 15 years after the premiere of her first critically acclaimed Las Vegas residency.

Celine and kids wear brand NUNUNU launched a new children's fashion brand CELINUNUNU in November 2018, featuring gender-neutral styles and a minimalistic colour palette.

2019 looks to be the start of a new era. Celine, who has been named L'Oréal's newest global spokesperson, will embark on her Courage World Tour in the fall, following the conclusion of her legendary Las Vegas residency. Celine debuted "Flying On My Own," a new upbeat, empowering track from her upcoming album, during her last show in Las Vegas.

The much-anticipated Courage World Tour began three months later, on September 18, in Celine's home province of Quebec, and will run until the fall of 2020, visiting nearly 100 cities worldwide.

Celine released her first English album in six years, "Courage," on November 15th, an eclectic album that represents Celine's new artistic direction. The album contains the hits "Imperfections," "Lying Down," and "Courage," which were all released on the same day as her massive world tour began.

A woman of destiny who is following her destiny.

Celine Dion has become a pop music legend, with one of the most powerful and moving voices ever heard, after more than 35 years of performing and recording. A genuine singer who sings from the heart. It's as simple and true as that - just like Celine.

MUSICAL INFLUENCES AND PERSONALITY

Dion is widely regarded as having one of the most influential voices in pop music. She calls herself a mezzo-soprano and sings in a classical manner with a three-octave range. Her music has been influenced by genres ranging from R&B to gospel to rock and classical, and she has received mixed reviews. Celine cites Barbra Streisand, Aretha Franklin, and Whitney Houston as vocal stylistic influences. She has been cited as an inspiration and influence on many of today's most popular singers, and she has worked with some of the world's most famous musicians.

THE CAUSE OF CELINE DION'S WEIGHT LOSS IS DISCLOSED

According to HelloMagazine, Celine Dion has always had a trim figure, but fans have questioned her slimmer frame since her husband's death in 2016.

The Think Twice hitmaker has never revealed how much weight she has lost in the years since, but she has previously stated that she feels "strong and feminine" after making some lifestyle changes.

Celine has previously stated that genetics play a significant role in her appearance. Previously, she told The Guardian: "I have been thin all my life. Nobody in my family is overweight."

Celine, on the other hand, is aware of her fans' concern for her health, telling ABC News in 2019: "It's true that I'm a little thinner. Everything's fine, nothing's wrong."

"I'm doing this for me. I want to feel strong, beautiful, feminine and sexy," she added to The Sun last year.

Her newfound love of ballet is one reason for her change in appearance. "I do [ballet] four times a week," she told People last year. "People say, 'She's a lot thinner,' but I'm working hard. I like to move and (weight loss) comes with it."

Dancing around on stage during her performances is undoubtedly another factor in her image transformation. Celine will perform at least six times per week and is preparing for another Las Vegas residency in November.

"Dancing has been in my DNA all of my life. It's a dream. And so hard!" She updated People.

Whatever she's doing to stay fit is benefiting her mental health. She told ABC News, "I feel stronger, more beautiful, more grounded. "That maturity brings this power and strength."

And Celine has a resolute message for those who judge her appearance, telling The Sun in January 2020: "If I like it, I don't want to talk about it. Don't bother. Don't take a picture. If you like it, I'll be there. If you don't, leave me alone."

CELINE DION'S EXCRUCIATING HEALTH BATTLE

According to HelloMagazine, Celine Dion has largely remained out of the spotlight since revealing in October 2021 that she was suffering from a debilitating health condition.

Due to her condition, the singer canceled her Las Vegas residency and postponed the North American and European legs of her Courage world tour. Celine revealed at the time that she was suffering from "severe and persistent muscle spasms," which had forced her to stop performing.

Fans are still concerned about Celine's health a year after her initial health update.

What is wrong with Celine Dion?

Several weeks after her diagnosis, Celine's sister, Claudette, told the French magazine Voici: "What's happening to her is sad. But it's not serious. Celine turns to me for advice and confides in me if something goes wrong. I know she's in good spirits."

HELLO! also spoke to Dr. Giuseppe Aragona, GP and health adviser for Online Prescription Doctor, back in April about the conditions that could cause the severe muscle spasms that have rendered Celine unable to perform.

"Muscle spasms are not usually a cause for concern and can occur because of a multitude of reasons, which can often make it tricky to pinpoint the problem," he explained. Stress, electrolyte imbalances, over-exercising, thyroid disease, or multiple sclerosis are all causes of muscle spasms, none of which Celine has revealed she suffers from.

I was really expecting that I'd be good to go by now, but I suppose I simply have to be more patient and follow the regimen that my doctors are prescribing, said Celine of her decision to cancel the North American leg of her tour in January.

When she announced that the European leg of her tour would also be rescheduled, she gave fans a ray of hope.

"The good news is that I'm getting better," she said. "But it's going very slow, and it's very frustrating for me," she added, clarifying that she was still experiencing some spasms.

Celine initially stated that she was postponing her Las Vegas show until March 22 due to "unforeseen medical symptoms," but that date has passed and there is still no word on her return to Sin City.

"Since my team and I have been working on our new program for the past eight months, I am utterly devastated that we won't be able to debut it in November, "At the time, she stated.

"Now, I have to focus on getting better... I want to get through this as soon as I can. I feel so horrible that I'm letting them down, and I'm especially sorry for disappointing all the fans who have been making their arrangements to travel to Las Vegas. - Celine"

CHAPTER THREE

AWARDS AND NET WORTH

AWARDS

1982

Yamaha World Popular Song Festival - Japan

Gold Medal – Yamaha World Song Festival, Tokyo Japan for Best Song – "Tellement j'ai d'amour pour toi"

Yamaha Symphony Orchestra Awards - Japan

Best Artist

1983

Félix Award - ADISQ Gala - Quebec, Canada

Best New Artist of the Year

Félix Award - ADISQ Gala - Quebec, Canada

Pop Album of the Year – "Tellement j'ai d'amour pour toi"

Félix Award - ADISQ Gala - Quebec, Canada

Quebec artist achieving the most success outside the province of Quebec

Félix Award - ADISQ Gala - Quebec, Canada

Female Vocalist of the Year

1984

Félix Award - ADISQ Gala - Quebec, Canada

Best Selling Album – "Les chemins de ma maison"

Félix Award - ADISQ Gala - Quebec, Canada

Female Vocalist of the Year

1985

Félix Award - ADISQ Gala - Quebec, Canada

Album of the Year – "Mélanie"

Félix Award - ADISQ Gala - Quebec, Canada

Best Selling Album of the Year – "Mélanie"

Félix Award - ADISQ Gala - Quebec, Canada

Female Vocalist of the Year

Félix Award - ADISQ Gala - Qucbec, Canada

Pop Song of the Year – "Une colombe"

Félix Award - ADISQ Gala - Quebec, Canada

Best Selling Single of the Year – "Une colombe"

1988

Eurovision Song Contest – Worldwide

First Prize for "Ne partez pas sans moi"

MetroStar Gala – Canada

Young Artist of the Year under 25 years of age

Félix Award - ADISQ Gala - Quebec, Canada

Best Live Performance of the Year for "Celine Dion"

Félix Award - ADISQ Gala - Quebec, Canada

Female Vocalist of the Year

Félix Award - ADISQ Gala - Quebec, Canada

Best Pop Song for "Incognito"

Félix Award - ADISQ Gala - Quebec, Canada

Quebec artist achieving the most success outside the province of Quebec – Francophone Market

1990

MuchMusic Video Awards – Canada

Best Video for "Can't Live with You, Can't Live without You " (duet with Billy – Newton Davis)

1991

Juno Awards – Canada

Album of the Year – "Unison"

Juno Awards – Canada

Female Vocalist of the Year

Félix Award - ADISQ Gala - Quebec, Canada

Quebec artist achieving the most success in a language other than French

1992

World Music Awards

World's Best selling Canadian Female Recording Artist of the Year

Juno Awards – Canada

Female Vocalist of the Year

Félix Award - ADISQ Gala - Quebec, Canada

Best Selling Album of the Year – "Dion chante Plamondon"

Félix Award - ADISQ Gala - Quebec, Canada

Quebec artist achieving the most success in a language other than French

Governor General's Awards

Honoured with a medal of recognition on Canada's 125th Birthday from the Governor General for her contribution to Canadian culture

MuchMusic Awards – Canada

Video Award for Best Adult Contemporary Video – "Je danse dans ma tête"

Academy Awards – USA

Best Song Written for a Motion Picture or Television – "Beauty and the Beast"

Golden Globe Awards – USA

To Alan Menken & Howard Ashman for Best Original Song for a Motion Picture – "Beauty and the Beast"

1993

Félix Award - ADISQ Gala - Quebec, Canada

Quebec artist achieving the most success outside the province of Quebec

Félix Award - ADISQ Gala - Quebec, Canada

Quebec artist achieving the most success in a language other than French

Billboard Awards – USA

Billboard International Creative Achievement Award

Grammy Awards – USA

Best Pop Performance by a Duo or Group with Vocal – "Beauty and the Beast"

Grammy Awards – USA

To Alan Menken & Howard Ashman for Best Song Written Specifically for a Motion Picture or for Television – "Beauty and The Beast"

Juno Awards – Canada

Female Vocalist of the Year

Juno Awards – Canada

Single of the Year – "Beauty and the Beast" (coincidentally nominated in the same category for "If You Asked Me To")

Juno Awards – Canada

Best Selling Francophone Album – "Dion chante Plamondon"

Juno Awards – Canada

Best Dance Recording – "Love Can Move Mountains" (Club Mix)

1994

Félix Award - ADISQ Gala - Quebec, Canada

Quebec artist achieving the most success outside the province of Quebec

Félix Award - ADISQ Gala - Quebec, Canada

Quebec artist achieving the most success in a language other than French

Félix Award - ADISQ Gala - Quebec, Canada

Female Artist of the Year

Juno Awards – Canada

Female Vocalist of the Year

Grammy Awards – USA

To David Foster & Jeremy Lubbock for Best Instrumental Arrangement Accompanying Vocal(s) – "When I Fall In Love"

1995

Ivor Novello Awards – UK

Song of the Year – "Think Twice"

Juno Awards – Canada

Album of the Year – "The Colour of My Love"

Juno Awards – Canada

Best Selling Album (Foreign or Domestic) – "The Colour of My Love"

World Music Awards

World's Best-Selling Canadian Female Recording Artist of the Year

Félix Award - ADISQ Gala - Quebec, Canada

Pop/rock Album of the Year – "D'eux"

Félix Award - ADISQ Gala - Quebec, Canada

Quebec artist achieving the most success outside the Province of Quebec

Félix Award - ADISQ Gala - Quebec, Canada

Most Popular Song of the Year – "Pour que tu m'aimes encore"

1996

Félix Award - ADISQ Gala - Quebec, Canada

Quebec artist achieving the most success outside the Province of Quebec

Félix Award - ADISQ Gala - Quebec, Canada

Best Selling Album of the Year – "D'eux"

Félix Award - ADISQ Gala - Quebec, Canada

Female Artist of the Year

Félix Award - ADISQ Gala - Quebec, Canada

Performance of the Year

Félix Award - ADISQ Gala - Quebec, Canada

Quebec artist achieving the most success in any language other than French

Juno Awards – Canada

Best Selling Francophone Album of the Year – "D'eux"

Médaille des Arts et Lettres (Medal of Arts and Letters) – France

Awarded the Médaille des Arts et Lettres from France's Minister of Culture recognizing her status as the best-selling French-language artist in history

MIDEM Awards – Europe

Award for combined European sales of over 10 million units in 1995

MIDEM Awards – Worldwide

Award for sales of over 4 million units worldwide for the album "D'eux"

IRMA Awards (Irish Recorded Music Awards) – Ireland

Best International Female Artist Album

Victoires de la musique – France

Best Song of the Year – "Pour que tu m'aimes encore"

Victoires de la musique – France

Best Francophone Artist

Trophée Radio France International / Conseil Francophone de la chanson – France

Awarded for the song "Pour que tu m'aimes encore"

VH1 Awards – USA

Artist of The Year

BAMBI Awards – Germany

Top International Pop Star of the Year

Japan Gold Disc Awards – Japan

International Music/Grand Prix Single Prize for "To Love You More"

World Music Awards – Worldwide

World's Best Selling Canadian Recording Artist of the Year

Malta Music Awards – Malta

Best Selling International Artist

1997

World Music Awards

World's Best Selling Pop Artist of the Year

World Music Awards

World's Overall Best Selling Recording Artist of the Year

World Music Awards

World's Best Selling Canadian Recording Artist of the Year

Félix Award - ADISQ Gala - Quebec, Canada

Album of the Year (Best Seller) – "Live à Paris"

Félix Award - ADISQ Gala - Quebec, Canada

Album of the Year (Pop Rock) – "Live à Paris"

Félix Award - ADISQ Gala - Quebec, Canada

Most Successful Quebecois Artist Outside Quebec

Félix Award - ADISQ Gala - Quebec, Canada

Most Successful Quebecois Artist in A Language Other Than French

Félix Award - ADISQ Gala - Quebec, Canada

Female Vocalist of the Year

Grammy Awards – USA

Album of the Year – "Falling Into You"

Grammy Awards – USA

Best Pop Album – "Falling Into You"

Grammy Awards – USA

To Diane Warren for Best Song Written Specifically for A Motion Picture or for Television – "Because You Loved Me"

NARM Awards – USA

1996/1997 Best Seller Award for Artist of the Year

NARM Awards – USA

1996/1997 Best Seller Award for Recording of the Year – "Falling Into You"

NARM Awards – USA

1996/1997 Best Seller Award for Pop Recording – "Falling Into You"

International Achievement in Arts Awards – USA

Entertainer of the Year for Distinguished Achievement in Music

Juno Awards – Canada

Female Vocalist of the Year

Juno Awards – Canada

Best Selling Francophone Album – "Live à Paris"

Juno Awards – Canada

Best Selling Album (Foreign or Domestic) – "Falling Into You"

Juno Awards – Canada

International Achievement Award

Pop Corn Music Awards – Greece

Best Album of the Year – "Falling Into You"

Pop Corn Music Awards – Greece

Best Female Singer of the Year

Irish Recorded Music Awards – Ireland

Best International Female Artist Album – "Falling Into You"

Coca-Cola Full Blast Music Awards – South Africa

Most Popular International Artist of 1996

Malta Music Awards – Malta

Best Selling Female International Artist

FM Select Diamond Awards – Hong Kong

Top Female International Artist

Amigo Awards – Spain

Best International Female Artist

National TV2 Awards – Denmark

Best International Female Artist

1998

American Music Awards – USA

Favourite Pop/Rock Female Artist

Performance Magazine Readers Poll Awards – USA

Best Pop Act

Golden Globe Awards – USA

To James Horner & Will Jennings for Best Original Song – "My Heart Will Go On"

Academy Awards – USA

To James Horner & Will Jennings for Best Original Song – "My Heart Will Go On"

BMI Pop Awards – USA

Song of the Year – "It's All Coming Back to Me Now"

VH1 Awards – USA

Best Female Artist

VH1 Awards – USA

Diva of the Year

VH1 Awards – USA

Artist of the Year

Billboard Music Awards – USA

Album of the Year – "Titanic"

Billboard Music Awards – USA

Female Album of the Year – "Let's Talk About Love"

Billboard Music Awards – USA

Soundtrack Album of the Year – "Titanic"

Billboard Music Awards – USA

Soundtrack Single of the Year – "My Heart Will Go On"

Billboard Music Awards – USA

Album Artist of the Year

Billboard Music Awards – USA

Adult Contemporary Artist of the Year

Japan Record Awards – Japan

Special Achievement, International Artist – "My Heart Will Go On"

Japan Gold Disc Award - Japan Grand Prix – Japan

Best International Pop Album of the Year – "Let's Talk About Love"

Japan Gold Disc Award - Japan Grand Prix – Japan

Artist of the Year – International music

Pop Corn Music Awards – Greece

Best Female Singer of the Year

Hungarian Record Industry Awards – Hungary

International Album of the Year – "Let's Talk About Love"

The Order of Canada

Appointed Officer of the Order of Canada for outstanding contribution to the world of contemporary music

National Order of Québec – Canada

Appointed Officer of the National Order of Québec

MuchMusic People's Choice Awards – Canada

Video Award for Favourite Canadian Artist

South African Music Awards – South Africa

Best Selling International Album – "Falling Into You"

AMIGO Awards – Spain

Best International Female Artist

World Music Awards

World's Best Selling Canadian Recording Artist of the Year

1999

Blockbuster Entertainment Awards – USA

Favourite Song from a Movie – "My Heart Will Go On" from Titanic

Grammy Awards – USA

Best Female Pop Vocal Performance – "My Heart Will Go On"

Grammy Awards – USA

Record of the Year – "My Heart Will Go On"

Grammy Awards – USA

To James Horner & Will Jennings for Song of the Year – "My Heart Will Go On"

Grammy Awards – USA

To James Horner & Will Jennings for Best Song Written for a Motion Picture or for Television – "My Heart Will Go On" from Titanic

Golden Globe Awards – USA

To Carol Bayer, David Foster, Alberto Testa & Tony Renis for Best Original Song from a Motion Picture – "The Prayer"

American Music Awards – USA

Favorite Female Pop/Rock Artist

American Music Awards – USA

Favorite Adult Contemporary Artist

American Music Awards – USA

Favorite Soundtrack – "Titanic"

People's Choice Awards – USA

Favorite Female Music Performer

Performance Magazine Awards - USA

To René Angélil for Personal Manager of the Year

Juno Awards – Canada

Female Vocalist of the Year

Juno Awards – Canada

Best Album – "Let's Talk About Love"

Juno Awards – Canada

Best Selling Album (Foreign or Domestic) – "Let's Talk About Love"

Juno Awards – Canada

Best Selling Francophone Album – "S'il suffisait d'aimer"

Juno Awards – Canada

International Achievement Award

Félix Award - ADISQ Gala - Quebec, Canada

Most Successful Quebecois Artist in A Language Other Than French

Walk of Fame – Canada

Inducted into Canada's Walk of Fame

Canadian Broadcast Hall of Fame – Canada

Inducted into the Canadian Broadcast Hall of Fame

Echo Awards – Germany

Most Successful International Female Artist

BAMBI Awards – Germany

For Sales of Over 10 million CDs in Germany, Austria and Switzerland

Japan Gold Disc Awards – Japan

Artist of the Year (International music category)

Japan Gold Disc Awards – Japan

Song of the Year (International music category) – "My Heart Will Go On"

Japan Gold Disc Awards – Japan

Pop Album of the Year – "These Are Special Times"

South African Music Awards – South Africa

Best Selling International Album – "Let's Talk About Love"

World Music Awards – Worldwide

World's Best-Selling Female Pop Artist

2001

American Music Awards – USA

Favorite Artist – Adult Contemporary

NRJ Music Awards – France

Francophone group/duo for the duet "Sous le vent" with Garou

2002

Billboard Latin Awards– USA

Special Award for "My Heart Will Go On" as the first English-language song to top Billboard's Hot Latin Tracks chart

Victoire de la musique – France

Original Song of the Year – "Sous le vent" (duet with Garou)

Félix Award – ADISQ Gala – Quebec, Canada

Most Successful Quebecois Artist in a Language Other Than French

Dragon Awards – Poland

Female Artist of the Year – International

2003

American Music Awards – USA (November)

Favorite Artist – Adult Contemporary

American Music Awards – USA (January)

Favorite Artist – Adult Contemporary

Arion Music Awards – Greece

Best Sales, International Album for "A New Day Has Come"

Radio Music Awards – USA

Artist of the Year - Adult Contemporary Radio

2004

Star on Hollywood Walk of Fame – USA

Diamond Award – World Music Awards

World's Best-Selling Female Artist of All Time

ELLA Awards – Society of Singers – USA

For Contribution to Music and Humanitarian and Community Support

Woman of the Year – Nevada Ballet Theatre – USA

For Significant Contribution to the Performing Arts

FIFI Awards – The Fragrance Foundation – USA

Fragrance of the Year – Women's Popular Appeal for "Celine Dion Parfums"

2005

Las Vegas Review Journal - The Best of Las Vegas – USA

Best Singer

2006

FIFI Awards – The Fragrance Foundation – USA

Best Packaging – Women's Popular Appeal for "Belong"

SOCAN Gala – Montreal, Quebec

Composition of "Tout près du bonheur" in Pop/Rock Music category (Celine Dion, Marc Dupré, Nelson Minville)

Las Vegas Review Journal - The Best of Las Vegas – USA

Best Singer

2007

Legend Award – World Music Awards

In recognition of a top recording artist for her global success and outstanding contribution to the music industry

Entertainer of the New Millennium – Nevada Commission on Tourism

For Contribution in the bettering of the quality of life for Nevada residents and for the immense success of "A New Day..."

Las Vegas Review Journal - The Best of Las Vegas – USA

Best All-Around Performer

Las Vegas Review Journal - The Best of Las Vegas – USA

Best Singer

Etoiles Chérie FM – France

Chérie FM of Honour for her long-standing career

2008

Best Selling Canadian Artist – World Music Awards

In recognition of being the top selling Canadian artist in 2008.

Honorary Félix Award – ADISQ Gala - Quebec, Canada

In recognition of having received more Félix awards than any other artist in the history of the gala.

Honorary Doctorate in Music - Laval University - Canada

In recognition of her personal and professional achievements.

Companion of the Order of Canada

Appointed "Companion of the Order of Canada" in recognition of her worldwide musical influence as well as for her commitment to numerous humanitarian causes.

Legion of Honour – L'Ordre National de la Légion d'Honneur

Appointed "Chevalier de la Légion d'Honneur" for her merits and contributions to France.

Walk of Fame – Poland

Inducted into Poland's Walk of Fame

NRJ Music Awards – France

Honorary Award - In recognition of her long-standing career

2012

BAMBI Awards — Germany

Entertainment Category — In Recognition of Her Long-Standing Musical Career.

SOCAN Gala — Montreal, Quebec

Composition of "Entre deux mondes" in Pop/Rock Music category (Celine Dion, Frederick Baron)

2013

Félix Award - ADISQ Gala - Quebec, Canada

Adult Contemporary Album of the Year - "Sans attendre"

Félix Award - ADISQ Gala - Quebec, Canada

Best-Selling Album of the Year - "Sans attendre"

GRAND PRIX - UNAC (Union nationale des auteurs compositeurs) – France

Song of the Year - "Parler à mon père"

2014

CBC Music Awards - Canada

Artist of the Year

2016

Billboard Music Award -USA

Icon Award

2017

Félix Award - ADISQ Gala - Quebec, Canada

Best Selling Album of the Year – "Encore un soir"

Félix Award - ADISQ Gala - Quebec, Canada

Album of the Year – Adult Contemporary - "Encore un soir"

2018

The Canadian Arts & Fashion Awards (CAFA) – Canada

International Style Icon Award

CELINE DION NET WORTH

Celine Dion is a well-known Canadian singer, actress, songwriter, and entrepreneur with an estimated net worth of $800 million. The powerful, technically accomplished vocals of Celine Dion are well-known. She is also respected for her impressive earning potential. Celine has earned $40 to $50 million in recent years from her various endeavors, with the majority of that income coming from a lucrative Las Vegas residency deal.

She has sold over 220 million albums worldwide and remains a popular live performer. Her Courage World Tour, which kicked off in September 2019, completely sold out all 52 North American dates. The European leg of the tour was on track to sell similarly well, but it was forced to be canceled due to the Coronavirus outbreak.

How much money does Celine Dion make from her Las Vegas show?

Celine began hosting a Las Vegas concert residency in March 2011. Between 2011 and 2019, the show grossed $250 million in ticket sales and other revenue. She performs 70 times per year and earns $500,000 PER PERFORMANCE. That works out to $35 million per year, making her by far the highest-paid performer in Las Vegas.

CHAPTER FOUR

QUOTES BY CELINE DION

Celine Dion Quotes on Passion

"Never say that your life is to be a singer. You want to sing because it's a part of your life. But if you don't succeed as a singer, it doesn't mean you don't have a life and it's over."

"I only record songs that touch me in some way, ones that I can relate to."

"In terms of music, I can try anything I want, even something that doesn't work at all, because I'm not putting my career in jeopardy."

"Don't make your career be your life. Let it be your passion. Let it bring you pleasure. But don't let it become your identity. You are so much more valuable than that."

"I don't just sing for free. It's my work. You're paid for what you do. And I work hard."

"I will perform 'My Heart Will Go On' for the rest of my life and it will always remain a very emotional experience for me."

"When I hear something that comes from me that makes me fall down off my chair, it's not often."

"I love to sing and perform. It is what I do and love. It completes my life."

"The first song that I ever recorded was written by my mother."

"I don't know if the camera likes me, but I do like the camera."

"When you're a parent, you sing better. It becomes a pure pleasure, rather than something I have to do."

Best Celine Dion Quotes

"There's no such thing as aging, but maturing and knowledge. It's beautiful, I call that beauty."

"Everything that I decide to do means something, otherwise, I don't do them."

"The only failure is not knowing how to be happy."

"If you follow your dreams, it means you follow your heart. If you do follow your heart, I don't think you can go wrong."

"When you are surrounded by children, the child in you comes back."

"It's the moment you think you can't, that you can."

"Life imposes things on you that you can't control, but you still have the choice of how you're going to live through this."

"The craziest thing I've done is cut my hair blonde and short a couple of years ago. And people reached out to me saying, 'Celine, you're one of the most stable things we have in our lives, don't do that. We want you the way you are'."

"I'm not in competition with anybody but myself. My goal is to beat my last performance."

"Your heart is pure, your soul is free. Be on your way, don't wait for me."

"At home, we don't listen to our music-we listen to other people's music. It keeps you attached to the show business world."

"I have shared my whole life. My private life and my show business life. It helps me actually to feel my songs and to go on with my dreams."

"I often buy myself presents. Sometimes I will spend $100,000 in one day in a posh boutique."

"I looked in the audience. There were no strangers. Everybody was singing and cheering and hugging. That was a beautiful picture to look at."

"I've never been cool - and I don't care."

"I have to say that when you tour the world, obviously, the jetlags and different hours and ways of living and traveling, a lot of hours in the plane, and you wake up in the morning and you're not quite sure where you are, and it is very tiring."

"I'm not going to be Rihanna. No one can be Rihanna except for Rihanna."

Celine Dion Quotes on Love

"Near, far wherever you are... you're here in my heart."

"Love comes to those who believe it, and that's the way it is."

"Love doesn't ask why, speaks from the heart, and never explains."

"Love can touch us one time

And last for a lifetime

And never let go till

We're gone."

Celine Dion Quotes on Family

"I think that life has a secret, and children hold that secret. Maybe it's not given to everybody to discover this thing."

"My child was not only carried by me, but by the universe."

"I'm passionate about my fans and my shows. But my biggest reward in the success that is my life are my husband and kids."

"I gave life, and that is beautiful."

"I'm so centered in feeling great about me that I can give great things to my son and my husband and my family."

"You've been my inspiration, through the lies you were the truth. My world is a better place because of you."

"I have become a housewife and there is no better job."

"I knew it was going to be the most extraordinary thing in my life, but how powerful it is, you can never know until you have a baby."

"It's really all about family, love and the children for me. I work at that every day."

"I want to be more successful as a mother than I am in show business."

Celine Dion Quotes on Success

"The hardest thing to find in life is balance; especially the more success you have, the more you look to the other side of the gate. What do I need to stay grounded, in touch, in love, connected, and emotionally balanced. Look within yourself."

"Don't be so familiar and so much into the details. Keep people dreaming. Close the window, and make them wonder."

"I worked really hard, and I surpassed myself... I didn't have, visually, what it took. I was not pretty, I had teeth problems, and I was very skinny. I didn't fit the mold."

"Golf is a search for perfection, for balance. It's about meditation and concentration. You have to use your hands and brain."

"I'm not looking for career attention, for more success, more money. I'm just singing songs I chose because I love them."

"My feet are definitely more grounded than before. And I know that I'm not holding onto a dream. I'm holding onto my life."

"Some people can't stand being alone. I love solitude and silence. But when I come out of it, I'm a regular talking machine. It's all or nothing for me."

"There's been nothing but discipline, discipline, discipline all my life."

"What do you say to taking chances?"

"I definitely would never go back to my 20s. The best is yet to come."

"I'll be a Quebecker-Canadian. I'm from Quebec, and every time I go to a country, I say that. It's my roots, my origins, and it's the most important thing to me."

"I started at 5 years old in the kitchen table with my family supporting me. I know where I'm from and I know exactly where I'm going."

CHAPTER FIVE

TRIBUTES TO RENÉ

"I understood that my career was in a way his masterpiece, his song, his symphony. The idea of leaving it unfinished would have hurt him terribly. I realized that if he ever left us, I would have to continue without him, for him."

Céline Dion

René arrives. He enters the room. Softly. Discreetly. He walks slowly, soundlessly. And yet, we see only him. In an instant, his presence completely changes the ambience. The mood becomes calm. Time stands still.

He shakes hands with every person there. Those whom he knows well, he hugs. He kisses them. Men and women alike. Without ever rushing through any sign of affection. Because he needs this as well. Just as much.

He does not look above or past people. He looks right into them. Right in their eyes. And his look is deeply perceptive. It plumbs the sincerity of who you are. You should also have a sincere, open look in your eyes. To maintain that gaze with the same sincerity. With the same intelligence.

René is an observer. A card player. He analyzes. He knows that every detail counts. He figures out all the hidden games. A man of great emotions, with a poker face.

René does not demand respect. He does better – he offers it. Because the most respected man in show business is the one who most respects others. His genius is in thinking of everything, without forgetting a single person.

Then he asks you how you're doing, in his paternal voice. His faint voice, which speaks loudly enough to inspire. He does not ask solely out of politeness. He asks sincerely, for real. And if you had not been feeling well, you already feel better.

The simple presence of René in a room makes everyone there feel more important. This is because the simple fact of his presence reminds us that the important thing is being together. This is what emanates from him. Family is the most important thing. People are important.

Never has one love counted for as much in someone's life as the love René has for Céline. And the love Céline has for René. The lover is no longer with us. The love, however, is forever here. In her. In their children. In everything her man loved. His love is everywhere.

René arrives. René arrives in heaven. An eternal leader, he has gone to check out the other side, to see if everything is alright. And if it isn't, it will be when we meet him again, that's for sure.

Thank you for everything, René.

Stéphane Laporte

REFERENCE

https://www.scribd.com/book/304218069/Celine-Dion-Biography-Life-and-Career?utm_medium=cpc&utm_source=google_search&utm_campaign=3Q_Google_DSA_NB_RoW&utm_term=&utm_device=c&gclid=CjwKCAiApve bBhAvEiwAe7mHSOlsZvsAjVY7GAOUg1-9uU5LjnDoW33J2ZiolSL00Sa8JachWpbryxoC2x MQAvD_BwE

https://www.celinedion.com/about/biography/

https://kidadl.com/quotes/celine-dion-quotes

https://www.hellomagazine.com/healthandbeauty/health-and-fitness/20220930152951/celine-dion-health-what-is-wrong-health-battle-explained/

https://www.celebritynetworth.com/richest-celebrities/singers/celine-dion-net-worth/

https://www.hellomagazine.com/healthandbeauty/health-and-fitness/20210917121985/celine-dion-health-weight-loss/

https://www.womansday.com/life/entertainment/g2151/celine-dion-facts/#:~:text=The%20singer%2C%20who%20never%20graduated,role%20in%20her%20massive%20career.

Printed in Dunstable, United Kingdom